K-9 Cops

by Meish Goldish

Consultant: Officer Daniel Lane
Waterford Police Department
Master Trainer, North American Police Work Dog Association
President, Connecticut Police Work Dog Association

New York, New York

Credits

Cover, © LukaTDB/Shutterstock, © John Roman Images/Shutterstock, © Ernest R. Prim/Shutterstock, and © Shannon Stapleton/Reuters/Newscom; 4L, © Jeffrey D. Alred/Deseret News; 4R, © Jeffrey D. Alred/Deseret News; 5, © Jeffrey D. Alred/Deseret News; 6, © Len Kadan/Shutterstock; 7, © Jeffrey D. Alred/Deseret News; 8L, © Alexsey/iStock; 8TR, © radarreklama/fotolia; 8BR, © James Brey/iStock; 9, © Kevin P Coughlin/ASSOCIATED PRESS; 10, Photo Courtesy of the Logan Haus Kennels; 11, © Rich Legg/iStock; 12, © Michael Ireland/fotolia; 13, Photo courtesy of Search Dog Foundation; 14, © Ted S. Warren/AP/Corbis; 15, © SEAN D. ELLIOT/THE DAY/ASSOCIATED PRESS; 16, © Glen Stubbe/ZUMA Press/Newscom; 17L, Photo courtesy of the Connecticut Police Work Dog Association; 17R, Photo printed with permission from The West Hartford News/Kathleen Schassler; 18–19, © andreiuc88/Shutterstock; 18, © MARK BUGNASKI/MLIVE.COM/Landov; 19, © Herb Woerpel/mlive.com/Landov; 20, Photo Courtesy of The Burton View; 21, © Image Point Fr/Shutterstock; 22L, © BETH A. KEISER/ASSOCIATED PRESS; 22R, © FEMA/Alamy Stock Photo; 23L, © MARCOCCHI GIULIO/SIPA/Newscom; 23R, © Paul Chiasson/ASSOCIATED PRESS; 24, © arindambanerjee/Shutterstock; 25, Courtesy Detective Anthony Fox/Jackson, Mississippi Police Department; 26, © Tom Nebbia/CORBIS; 27, Photo Courtesy of the Portage Police Department; 28T, © Tom Vickers/Splash/Newscom; 28BL, © evp82/iStock; 28BM, Photo courtesy of Ruffwear Performance Dog Gear; 28BR, © mehmettorlak/iStock; 29L, © Leonard Zhukovsky/Shutterstock; 29T–B, © Katarzyna Bialasiewicz/Dreamstime; © pickingpok/iStock; © davidsansegundo/Shutterstock; © Ivan Cholakov/Shutterstock.

Publisher: Kenn Goin
Editor: Jessica Rudolph
Creative Director: Spencer Brinker
Photo Researcher: We Research Pictures, LLC

Library of Congress Cataloging-in-Publication Data

Names: Goldish, Meish, author.
Title: K-9 cops / by Meish Goldish.
Description: New York, NY : Bearport Publishing, [2016] | Series: Police: search & rescue! | Includes bibliographical references and index.
Identifiers: LCCN 2015040008| ISBN 9781943553136 (library binding) | ISBN 1943553130 (library binding)
Subjects: LCSH: Police dogs—Juvenile literature. | Rescue dogs—Juvenile literature.
Classification: LCC HV8025 .G653 2016 | DDC 363.2/3— dc23
LC record available at http://lccn.loc.gov/2015040008

For more information, write to Bearport Publishing Company, Inc., 45 West 21st Street, Suite 3B, New York, New York 10010. Printed in the United States of America.

10 9 8 7 6 5 4 3 2 1

Contents

Trapped Below!

One afternoon in December 2014, Kollin Bailey was flying a kite in a park close to his home in Utah. The boy didn't notice an open **manhole** in the grass. When he accidentally stepped into the hole, he fell 10 feet (3 m)! For a moment, the boy lay **unconscious**. When he woke, he was in pain—and scared. He screamed for help. However, the sound of nearby cars drowned out his cries.

Kollin Bailey with his mother

The manhole that Kollin fell into, with its cover

When Kollin didn't return home after four hours, his worried mother called 9-1-1. The West Valley City Police Department immediately sent out a **search party**. The search party included Sergeant (Sgt.) Shane Matheson and his **canine** partner, a bloodhound named Copper. The dog wouldn't need to hear Kollin's cries for help. Why? **Search-and-rescue dogs** rely on their incredible sense of smell to find missing people.

Sgt. Shane Matheson and Copper

Police officers have been using bloodhounds to search for missing people for more than 200 years.

Following the Scent

Sgt. Matheson asked Kollin's parents for some of the boy's belongings. The officer gave these items—a bike and a bed pillow—to Copper to sniff. By smelling them, the bloodhound learned the missing boy's **scent**. Then, the canine headed toward the park, sniffing the ground along the way. Sgt. Matheson followed closely behind. He carefully watched Copper's movements and scanned the surrounding area for the missing boy.

Bloodhounds sniff the ground when they search for missing people.

After 20 minutes of searching, Copper led his human partner to the manhole. Sgt. Matheson peered inside. Kollin was found! The boy had a broken arm, scratches, and bruises, but the quick rescue saved his life. Kollin's father said, "My son wouldn't be here with us today if we didn't have those **K-9 units** and great police officers."

The term *K-9* means the same as *canine*. K-9 often refers to a working dog, such as one that helps the police.

After being treated for a broken arm, Kollin got to spend time with Sgt. Matheson and Copper.

Searching Up and Down

Copper helped find Kollin by **trailing** the boy's scent. How is that possible? Every person **sheds** tiny skin **cells** all day long—about 40,000 cells per minute! Each cell has the person's scent on it. The **microscopic** cells float in the air until they fall to the ground.

German shepherd

Labrador retriever

Doberman pinscher

Common dog **breeds** used by police include bloodhounds, German shepherds, Labrador retrievers, and Doberman pinschers. These breeds are strong, energetic, and have an especially good sense of smell.

Search dogs may trail the scent of skin cells by sniffing the ground, the air, or both. Police dogs are able to follow scents almost anywhere—on city streets, in woods and swamps, or even on snowy mountains. Canines can pick up a person's scent as far as 3 miles (4.8 km) away!

A dog's sense of smell is about 1,000 times better than a person's!

Lots of Jobs

Police dogs can do more with their noses than just sniff out missing people. The K-9 unit for the Fayette County Sheriff's Department in West Virginia has several dogs that have different jobs. In addition to rescuing people in danger, the dogs track down criminals who are on the run from police. They also find hidden bombs and **illegal** drugs.

Each dog in a K-9 unit is paired with a police officer, who is the canine's **handler**.

The Fayette County Sheriff's Department recently received a new police dog named Bane. The dog is training to search for criminals and illegal drugs, and is partnered with Sgt. T.N. Mooney.

Just as humans leave behind scents, the **chemicals** that are used to make bombs and drugs leave behind scents, too. When police officers think that illegal substances may be hidden somewhere, K-9s are called in to sniff around. Officers may direct their K-9 partners to search a car on a street or a bag at an airport. Without the work of a K-9 unit, some illegal substances would never be found.

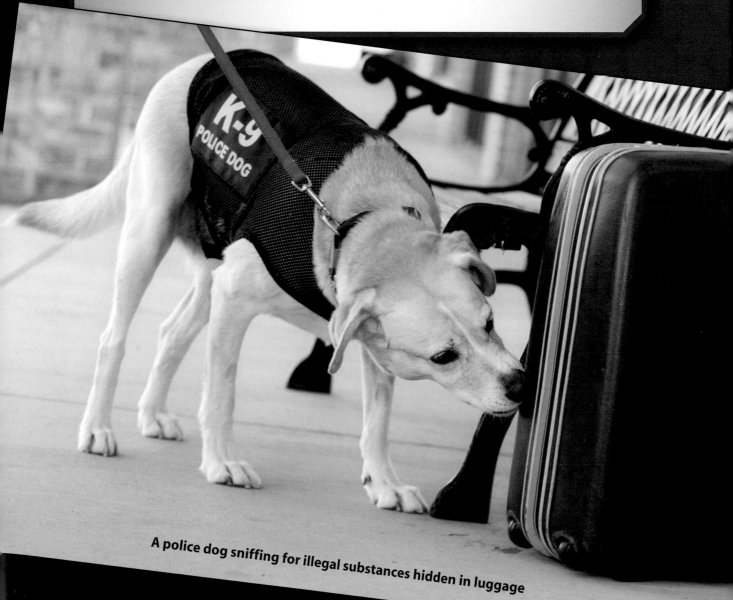

A police dog sniffing for illegal substances hidden in luggage

Learning the Game

No matter what the job, both K-9 cops and dogs have to first go through training. Often, a special **instructor** works with a dog before it is paired with an officer. The instructor teaches the dog many things, such as how to search. She may start off by running away from the dog and ducking behind a tree. The dog's **instinct** is to chase and find her.

Instructors teach search dogs to give a signal, such as sitting or barking, when they find something or someone.

The instructor may then hide the dog's favorite toy. The dog is taught a **command**, such as "Go find." The canine searches for the toy based on its scent. After finding it, the instructor rewards the dog with **praise**, a treat, or a toy. Over time, the dog learns to find people based on scent. The training is serious, but to the dog it's a fun game of hide-and-seek!

This dog found its instructor hidden in a barrel during training and is being rewarded with playtime.

Becoming Partners

After most of the dog's training is complete, it is paired with an officer. In special classes, the officer learns how to work with the dog. Cops are taught how to keep their dogs calm and **focused**. On the job, a dog may hear loud noises from trucks and helicopters. Staying calm in these stressful situations is very important.

Officers learn how to keep their dogs calm around crowds of people.

Officers also learn how to read small clues that tell them if their K-9 partner is confused, tired, hurt, or **distracted**. For instance, the dog may start to walk slowly or carry its ears or tail in a different position if it is tired. The officer then knows to take a break. No matter how the dog behaves, an officer learns to remain patient and gentle at all times.

Police officers take classes for several weeks or months to learn how to handle their dogs. After classes end, officers continue to do training exercises with their dogs every week for as long as the two are paired up.

Saving Animals

In addition to learning to work with their K-9 partners, some cops also get trained in animal **first aid**. This allows the cops to help their dog partners—or even somebody's pet—if the animal needs immediate medical help. In 2012, K-9 Officer Thomas Lazure of West Hartford, Connecticut, used his first-aid skills when he responded to a call about a choking dog.

In an animal first aid class, police officers practice on stuffed animals. The officers learn how to stop bleeding, apply bandages, and other life-saving skills.

When Officer Lazure arrived at the scene, he found a Shih-Tzu named Harry in trouble. His owners explained that the dog had started choking while chewing on a **rawhide**. The dog couldn't breathe, and time was running out. Officer Lazure performed the **Heimlich maneuver** by quickly pressing several times on the dog's rib cage. Soon, the rawhide loosened from the dog's throat. Harry could breathe again!

Harry the Shih-Tzu

Officer Thomas Lazure with his K-9 partner, Jett

Deep in the Woods

Sometimes, police handlers and their search dogs have to work long hours under difficult conditions. In May 2015, Deputy Ben Haas of the Allegan County Sheriff's Department in Michigan and his canine partner, Medo, were sent to look for Preston Johnson. The two-year-old had disappeared from his yard on a cold, rainy night. His parents feared that he was lost in the woods nearby.

Preston had been playing in his family's yard when he wandered away.

Deputy Haas and Medo searched the area around Preston's home. Hours passed with no sign of the boy. The deputy worried that Preston might have gotten hurt or even drowned in a nearby pond. Finally, at 4 A.M., Medo caught the boy's scent. Not long after, Deputy Haas spotted Preston deep in the woods—calmly playing in the mud. "He sat right there, smiled, and waved," the officer said. The boy even asked if he could pet the officer's dog!

Deputy Haas and Medo

 Several other K-9 teams, as well as a search helicopter, took part in the effort to find Preston. After being found, the boy was treated for scratches and poison ivy rashes on his arms and legs but was otherwise okay.

Getting Help

Police K-9 teams have many skills. Yet sometimes they need help from other emergency responders. This was the case for Officer Tony Greenway and his canine partner, Knox, of the Burton Police Department in Michigan. In April 2012, they were included in a search party that was sent to look for an elderly man who had disappeared from his home.

Officer Greenway and his K-9 partner, Knox

Working in freezing winds, Knox followed the man's scent to a wooded swamp. Soon, the dog signaled to Officer Greenway that the man was somewhere behind a **thicket**. However, the swamp was so **dense** with trees and bushes that the police couldn't see or get to him. To help, local firefighters were called to the scene. Fortunately, the firefighters had special equipment, including a **thermal imaging camera**, that allowed them to locate and rescue the man.

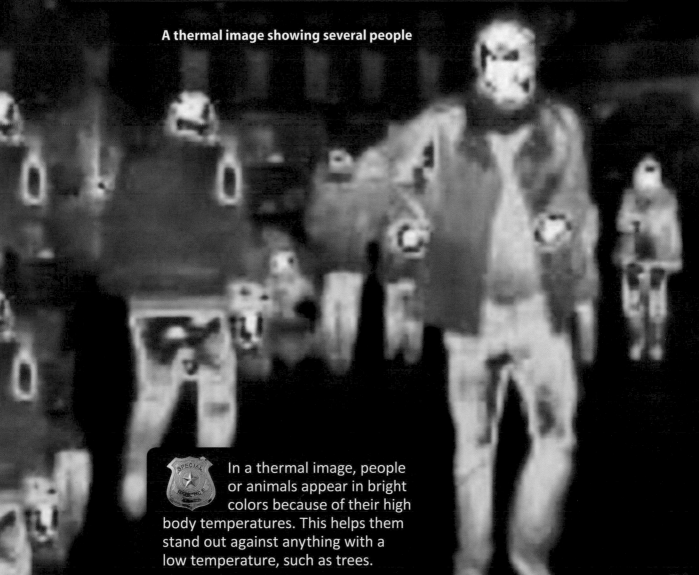

A thermal image showing several people

In a thermal image, people or animals appear in bright colors because of their high body temperatures. This helps them stand out against anything with a low temperature, such as trees.

The Biggest Search Ever

The largest K-9 search in U.S. history began on September 11, 2001. That day, **terrorists** flew planes into two **skyscrapers** in New York City. When the buildings burned and **collapsed**, police K-9 units from around the world rushed to the scene to search for **survivors**.

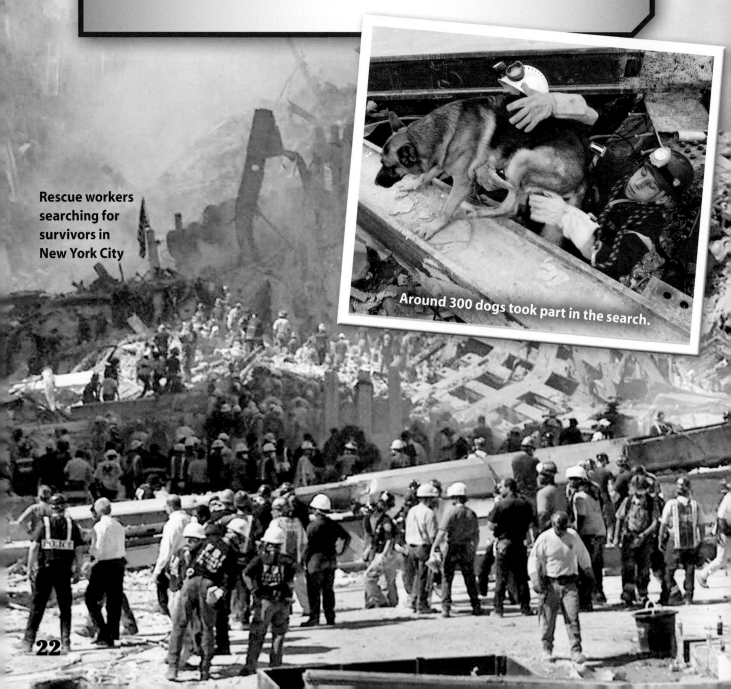

Rescue workers searching for survivors in New York City

Around 300 dogs took part in the search.

James Symington, a Canadian police officer, arrived with his canine partner, Trakr. Officer Symington led his German shepherd to an area filled with broken glass and twisted steel. After hours of sniffing the smoky air, Trakr signaled a spot to his human partner. Officer Symington told firefighters to search the area. The firefighters dug in the **rubble** and found Genelle Guzman-McMillan, an office worker who had been trapped for 24 hours. Thanks to Trakr and Symington, she survived.

Officer Symington and Trakr at the site of the disaster

Instead of finding the scent of one specific person, some search dogs are trained to pick up the scent of any person who may be buried under a collapsed building.

Genelle Guzman-McMillan

23

Partners Helping Partners

K-9 cops and their partners form such a strong bond that they will risk their lives for each other. One day in February 2015, Detective Anthony Fox of the Jackson Police Department in Mississippi was working with another officer when he saw in the distance that his parked police car had caught on fire. Even worse, the detective's K-9 partner, Alpha, was trapped inside the car!

A police car on fire

Detective Fox and the other officer sprinted down the road. Yet, when they reached the car, the door wouldn't budge! Alpha barked and barked as flames poured out of the vehicle. The officers pulled with all their might. Finally, the front door opened and Alpha jumped out.

Detective Fox had no problem risking his life for his dog. "I'll lay my life down for him," he said. "I know he would lay his life down for me."

Detective Anthony Fox with Alpha

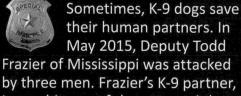
Sometimes, K-9 dogs save their human partners. In May 2015, Deputy Todd Frazier of Mississippi was attacked by three men. Frazier's K-9 partner, Lucas, bit one of the men and then all three attackers ran away.

A Special Pair

K-9 cops don't just work with their dog partners. Often, they live with them, too. When they are off duty, an officer and his or her canine relax and play together at home. By sharing free time, the pair's friendship and trust is strengthened, which helps them on the job.

A K-9 cop must love dogs and have patience with them, both at work and at home.

In Portage, Indiana, Officer Wendell Hite has a K-9 partner named Si. The dog lives with Officer Hite's family. The two have been partners for only about a year, but the dog is already like another member of the family. The officer says, "It's like having your kid, your best buddy."

In 2015, Officer Hite and his partner Si found five-year-old Maleyah after she got lost near her home.

After a search dog becomes too old to work, it often lives with its handler or with another loving family who will care for it.

K-9 Cops' Equipment

K-9 cops and their dog partners use special equipment when working. Here is some of their gear.

A *vest* identifies the dog as a police K-9.

A *leash* or *lead* is used during some searches to keep the dog within range of its handler.

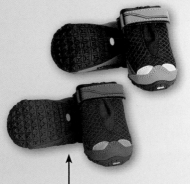

Boots or *paw mitts* protect the dog's paws when searching on rocky or cold ground or in an area with sharp objects such as broken glass or twisted metal.

Toys such as tennis balls may be given to search dogs as a reward after they find someone.

A *first-aid kit* has bandages and other medical items that may be needed if a person or dog is injured during a search.

A *flashlight* is used during searches in the dark.

A *two-way radio* allows an officer to stay in touch with other members of the search team.

A *helicopter* may be used to fly a K-9 team to a search area, or to fly a rescued person out of the area for medical help.

Glossary

breeds (BREEDZ) types of dogs

canine (KAY-nine) a member of the dog family

cells (SELZ) basic, very tiny parts of a person, animal, or plant

chemicals (KEM-uh-kuhlz) natural or human-made substances

collapsed (kuh-LAPST) fell down or caved in

command (kuh-MAND) an order given by someone to do something

dense (DENSS) very thick

distracted (diss-TRAK-tid) having one's attention or concentration drawn away

first aid (FURST AYD) care given to an injured or sick person in an emergency before he or she is treated by a doctor

focused (FOH-kuhsst) concentrating completely on something

handler (HAND-lur) someone who works with animals

Heimlich maneuver (HIME-lik muh-NOO-vur) an emergency action performed on a choking person or animal to force an object out of the windpipe

illegal (i-LEE-guhl) against the law

instinct (IN-stingkt) knowledge and behavior that an animal is born with and doesn't have to learn

instructor (in-STRUHK-tur) a teacher

K-9 units (KAY-nine YOO-nits) teams of police dogs and the officers who handle them

manhole (MAN-hohl) a covered hole in the street or ground that leads to sewers or underground pipes

microscopic (mye-kruh-SKOP-ik) extremely tiny; able to be seen only with a microscope

praise (PRAYZ) enthusiastic words of approval

rawhide (RAW-hyde) a treat for a dog to chew on

rubble (RUHB-uhl) pieces of broken concrete, bricks, and other building materials

scent (SENT) a smell or odor

search-and-rescue dogs (surch-and-RESS-kyoo DAWGZ) dogs that find people who are missing

search party (SURCH PAR-tee) a group organized to look for someone who is missing

sheds (SHEDZ) loses something from the body, such as fur or cells

skyscrapers (SKYE-*skray*-purz) very tall buildings

survivors (sur-VYE-vurz) people who live through a disaster or horrible event

terrorists (TERR-ur-ists) people who use violence and threats to achieve their goal

thermal imaging camera (THUR-muhl IM-ij-ing KAM-uh-ruh) a machine that locates a person or animal based on heat given off by the body

thicket (THIK-it) a very thick growth of bushes, trees, or other plants

trailing (TRAYL-ing) following the smell of a person or animal

unconscious (uhn-KON-shuhss) not awake; not able to see, feel, or think, often as the result of a serious illness or accident

Bibliography

American Rescue Dog Association. *Search and Rescue Dogs: Training the K-9 Hero.* New York: Howell Book House (2002).

Plum, Jennifer. *Careers in Police Departments' Search and Rescue Units (Careers in Search and Rescue Operations).* New York: Rosen (2003).

Snovak, Angela Eaton. *Guide to Search and Rescue Dogs.* Hauppauge, NY: Barron's (2004).

Read More

Blake, Kevin. *City Cops (Police: Search & Rescue!).* New York: Bearport (2016).

Goldish, Meish. *Ground Zero Dogs (Dog Heroes).* New York: Bearport (2013).

McGinty, Alice B. *Detector Dogs: Sniffing Out Trouble (Dogs Helping People).* New York: PowerKids Press (2003).

Ruffin, Frances E. *Police Dogs (Dog Heroes).* New York: Bearport (2005).

Learn More Online

To learn more about K-9 cops, visit
www.bearportpublishing.com/PoliceSearchAndRescue

Index

About the Author

Meish Goldish has written more than 200 books for children.
His book *Animal Control Officers to the Rescue* was a Children's Choices
Selection in 2014. He lives in Brooklyn, New York.